THE BEE HUT

THE BEE HUT

Dorothy Porter

Black Inc.

Published by Black Inc.,
an imprint of Schwartz Media Pty Ltd
37–39 Langridge Street
Collingwood VIC 3066 Australia
email: enquiries@blackincbooks.com
http://www.blackincbooks.com

Poems in this collection have appeared in the *Age*, *Agenda*, *Australian
Author*, *Australian Book Review*, *Australian Literary Review*, *The Best Australian
Poems 2003*, *2004*, *2005* and *2007* (Black Inc.), *The Best Australian Poetry
2006* and *2008* (University of Queensland Press), *Eureka Street*, *Heat*,
Island, *Meanjin*, *Overland*, *Over There: Poems from Singapore and Australia*,
Voices and *Wet Ink*.

The National Library of Australia Cataloguing-in-Publication entry:

Porter, Dorothy Featherstone, 1954–2008.

The bee hut / Dorothy Porter.

ISBN: 9781863954464 (pbk.)

A821.3

Book design by Thomas Deverall
Printed in Australia by Griffin Press

Contents

FOREWORD

Dorothy Porter never went anywhere without a volume of poetry. Whether to the local coffee shop or to Antarctica, a book of poems, and often several, travelled with her. She counted reading poetry among her greatest pleasures and her greatest blessings.

Her own poetry glows and shimmers with a lifetime of reading and this volume is no exception. All the poems, with the exception of the Freak Songs and a couple of others, were written in the last almost-five years of her life. It was a period of great happiness and satisfaction; the best, according to Dorothy, she had known. She produced a large body of new poetry, including her verse novel *El Dorado*; there were her collaborations with musicians Jonathan Mills, Paul Grabowsky and Tim Finn, and her work on the film of *The Eternity Man*, directed by Julien Temple. She was aware of a new depth to the way she inhabited her days, and often spoke about this. Always captivated by the wonder of existence, in the last years of her life Dot learned to live each moment as it occurred, to linger and dwell. She delighted in the everyday: home, family, friends, work, our cat; and she delighted in our travels, vividly represented in this collection, to Africa, Antarctica, the Great Barrier Reef, Uluru, London and New York. She acknowledged her good fortune several times each day.

Every few weeks during 2004 when she was undergoing treatment for breast cancer, Dot would spend the weekend with her friend Robert on his farm. She loved the country air, the birds, the quiet, the glimpse of the ocean on the horizon, and she was fascinated by the old hut, not far from the house, which had become home to a colony of bees.

The bee hut became a metaphor for these last years of her life – overwhelmingly healthy years, I should add. She marvelled at the bees, as she had always marvelled at life, but she was also aware of the danger amid the sweetness and beauty.

It was not the same, as she writes in one of the poems here, after she was first diagnosed with cancer. But as these poems show, Dorothy Porter saturated every moment with life right up to the end; her last poem, 'View from 417', was written in her hospital room on 26 November 2008, two weeks before she died. In *The Bee Hut* she has left behind a volume of poetry to travel with us through the days and years ahead.

Andrea Goldsmith

HEAD OF ASTARTE

EGYPT

The most powerful presence
is absence.

When the pyramid dissolves
you will keep
its shadow. its deep rich space.
in you.

Today you are strung,
shivering, with a haunted history.

You are singing dying songs
that hurt. but make you.

Perhaps in Egypt's death
is your salvation.

Its wailing gods. Its red
heart of desert. Its river
flowing like a stinging
harvest. Cling
and grow you richly.

Bless Egypt.
Bless her passing.

ON READING E.M. FORSTER'S
GUIDE TO ALEXANDRIA

'The best way of seeing it is to wander aimlessly about.'
—E.M. FORSTER

Imagine a city
where it's mostly
'imagine'

imagine a city, the story goes,
where one minute you're a bride
in your own wedding procession

next minute
the ground coughs and collapses
engulfing and delivering you

dusty and astonished
into the embalmed arms
of Alexander's equally astonished
lost corpse
lying gilded in a forgotten catacomb
under the traffic fumes.

Imagine a city where closeted
Mummy's Boy Morgan under Pompey's Pillar
feasts on erotic love for the first time

now imagine a city
with sexually-healed flâneur Forster
taking your elbow

through the seedy Rues
to light candles, cigarettes and the poet's best whisky
with Cavafy

imagine afterwards
to wind down from all that smoke, stoicism and intoxicating talk
you do the Greco-Roman Museum

and vulnerable still
you let the tomb terracotta statuettes
do your head in

because Morgan calls them
'the loveliest things in the museum'
because you're still unsteady with flesh-lambent poetry

because. because. because.
nothing lasts
not Forster. not Cavafy's eloquent doomed mediocrities. not you.

Now your aimless, wandering imagination
is shivering with the memory germ's fever
caught for the rest of your life

from this mercilessly contagious
imaginary city.

PLEASURE

After the Cleopatra exhibition, British Museum

Is it the bite
of a sighing crocodile?

All your voluptuous
bleeding incense
come at once?

I have travelled its Silk Road
with my curtains drawn,
hearing
its lurching mirages
shiver among the stones
and nettles
of its gorgeous desert.

WINE

Scorched through the journey of every slow sip
is the intimate memory
of Calvary.

The sponge dipped
in rough red
at the end of a spear.

That gift
from strangers
before they thoughtfully break your legs.

You must learn from dying gods
and gracefully render to the comfort
of intoxication.

Even the gibbering homicidal troll
under every life's bridge
can be stalled with a drink.

HEAD OF ASTARTE

Goddess in the London antiquities shop window,
whose starry name once soared,
how can your null and void terracotta head
shore me against my ruin?

I want to steal you from the underworld,
graft you like a juicy cutting of Orpheus
graft you like a seeding amulet
to the strings of my right hand.

Guide me through this bloody desert
of parching modernity.
Let's blow down the old straw god
draped in pious brutality.

Instead of adoring you like this
in furtive powerless bliss.

AENEAS REMEMBERS DOMESTIC BLISS

We were never married, Dido.
Cease weeping, let me leave and agree
we both knew real spouses.

Even as the ghost of my precious wife passed
through my clutching arms like mist
I swear on my soul I could *taste* her.

O the scorch of lost Trojan mornings
in our rumpled bed with bread, figs
and, yes, honey!

I could taste honey
as if every bee in Troy
had made her phantom its swarming hive.

Of course I will miss you.
But release us both from this futile tar-pit
and accept we were never married

yes, my divided heart rears for you
mourning already the smell of your flushed skin
and the sting of your green fire eyes

but we were never married
and your ghost – such threats! –
will keep its roost and never come

looking for me through
my next awful war, next sacked city
to flood my drought mouth in honey – or poison.

We were never married, Dido.
Believe me, I'm sad too that you can't
sweeten me and I can't comfort you.

THE LOVELY NIGHT. THE ROTTING SHIP

After Yannis Ritsos

The night they brought the aged Argo
    back to Corinth.

Torches. The procession
    through the nocturnal whispers
    of spring flowers.

The lovely night. The rotting ship.

An owl hoots
    across the derelict deck
    across the hallowed place
    (eaten through. rowlock lost)
    where Orpheus sat and sang.

The temple. The priests chanting
to miraculous memories.

The sleek young men dance
with the hairless grace
of mincing boys
who've never raised an oar
or a sweat.

An old sailor's rusty remembering
back
    squeaks like a baleful bat.

He spits at the ground.
  Then moves off
  to piss behind
  a black tree.

WALKING ON WATER

From one memory
the murk clears –

the nettles and rubbish
and low tide stench
of the Sea of Galilee
bathed in powdery glare

then glimpsed on a balcony
in a derelict building
a grubby solitary monk –

was he drunk or demented?

At eighteen
I made these judgements wildly
with a wincing lack
of charity –

but I remember clearly
the monk clattering about
in a suspicious mess
of empty bottles.

I was already at the alluring
beginning
of giving up religion
for a solemn and selfish
sense
of my own vocation –

I was glad to leave
the monk behind me.

I knew. I believed
ahead somewhere
in that white smelly morning
was the rippling shadow
of a fresh young god –

walking on water.

CAESAREA

The Mediterranean lifts
its barnacled blue arm
and throws you
a Roman coin.

It isn't beautiful.
Neither are you.
But you pray
its sea-roughed Emperor
will somehow benignly
see you through.

The gold-melt moon.
The aroma of gritty six a.m.
Turkish coffee.
Harsh warm Hebrew
pounding the air
like a confounding family
squabble.
The marooned marble column
on which you dry
your shabby old towel.

This glittering port city.
A sophisticated paradise.
Where Pontius Pilate thirsted
for the humanity
of face-saving lies.

You are only eighteen.
But thousands of years
of brackish Biblical history
sweep into you
and catch
like a thousand sharp
glass beads.

Sometimes a new place
has the ferocity of a gale
ripping the calm
off a safe harbour
making the drowned bells peel
Hallelujah
for all your future
false prophets
and glorious. glorious.
lost gods.

THE ENCHANTED ASS

BLACKBERRIES

I can't shake
that ghost-town pub
whistling empty-bottled
through its black windows,
and its strangled verandahs
creaking with a terrifying
ancient thirst
under a two-storey coat
of bristling blackberry.

Is it taunting me
with the dancing skeleton
tune
of my own life's mystery
struggling for rhythm
and lyrics?

I hold in my hand
the greedy, bleeding
pen
that has always
gorged itself.

The bliss-mouthed
gluttony miracle –
that stained Keats
grape-purple
that had cynical Byron
reeling on the ceiling –
when the plump berries
sing
and your pen slashes ahead
like a pain-hungry prince
hacking through
the bramble's dragon teeth
to the heart's most longed-for
comatose, but ardently ready
princess.

THE ENCHANTED ASS

So tender is the Queen of Fairies'
mouth
   on all your unsleeping parts

her kiss
   arrives
      like summery moonlight

her kiss is the mole's bliss
the blind
   blinding way

her green magic breaks in you
   like a warm storm

   you grow
      ears, tail,

   and a hee-hawing
      lightning.

A WALK IN KENSINGTON GARDENS

Solitude is where writers
chatter best

a soothing static –
the ambulatory, admit it, *happy*
ticking over

like this afternoon
in the sweet green cold London
spring
I watch a tall grey heron
stomping down its reed nest
that's sprouting everywhere
like garden-sheared hair

and all my living
and all my dead
run up my arms
like squirrels.

THE SILVER BRACELET

We were lost.
The map was a useless tease.
The afternoon was golden-green
cold.
It was old Ireland
after all.

Things happened that afternoon.
The dwarf at the door.
The strange dirty man on a bike
with an impossibly narrow face.
All gave false directions
to what we were so doggedly dreamily
looking for.

We pushed through an old gate
into a meadow
dancing with green light.
And found
the stone circle
so clearly, so mundanely
marked on the map.
Lichen-tipped, warm
as if squirming
with old friendly blood
the stones stood.

I can't remember how long
we stayed.
We danced around the stones
and took photos.
I still remember
the thin tune playing
in my charmed head.

On the ferry back to Holyhead
my bare wrist pinged
where my silver bracelet used to be.

Was it just something superstitious
young Yeats said
that made me believe
the fairies had taken
the silver bracelet
instead of me?

THE HOUSE

Is this what middle age
does to the imagination,
setting up haunted
house
in every idling cranny?

It's time I sent
my own premature ghost
scarpering
to a cobwebbed nunnery.

AFTER BRUEGEL

Let me join the frilled and flying
damned

and live vivid
as a wet dog.

THREE SONNETS

I. Is it not the thing?

After Byron

Trying to get a gutless friend
to get it
Byron wrote
Is it not life, is it not the thing?

He was praising the bawdy
spurt
of his own poem, his own
ballsy Don Juan.

Every poet wants to write the poem
that penetrates
with the ice-cold shock
of the Devil's prick.

The poem that will fuck you awake
or kill you.

II. What a plunge!

After Woolf

This morning the street
stings
like salt in a happily healing
wound.

A memory breaks under
your ribs
and plunges you
in turbulent sweet water.

Life is so dangerous,
but this morning you can take
the wave
right to the sparkling shore.

You can bear knowing
the street will one day dump you.

III. Beautifully bonkers

After Blake

Blake's burning Bow
turns and turns
in your inadequate trembling
hands.

What holy war
are you trembling for?
What purging dazzling madness
are you raising?

You squirm in paradox.
Hell today.
Paradise tomorrow.
It's all bliss and grist.

Or is it just those Arrows of Desire
spiking your drink again?

BLUEBOTTLES

In living there is always
the terror
of being stung

of something
coming for you
on the unavoidable wave.

In living there is always
the terror
of the alien boneless
thing

of something
blue
coming for you
from the blue and salty sea
spat
on your bare and shrinking
skin.

In living there is always
the terror
of the poison finding
your heart

of something
whose stingers
will stretch over you
like stars
with an ancient burning
patience.

THINGS

I.M. Ruth Tedeschi

Wafting
    half hallucinating
        with brain fatigue
through Berlin's massive
        Pergamon Museum
I think
    how strange. how sobering.
    that our things
        outlive us.

Whether it's the gleaming
      loot
of gold jewellery
    and silver plate
or the splash
      of vivid, intimate
          usefulness
in the broken
    ceramic jug.

Things
    outlive our sweetest
       most durable friends
things
     stolidly, persistently
      outlive our wildest
         loves
where we fling ourselves
into the heart
   of the black spitting fire
and declare
  we'll live here
      forever.

We bury our friends
we sink in their clay
        and weep.
We walk –
  in time –
    dripping wet
     with remorseless
      common sense
    out of love's fabulising
        flame.

It's just our things
   that survive
dissolving in the end
even the most sticky
  of our clutching
    smudges.

POEMS: JANUARY–AUGUST 2004

For Andy with love

THE NINTH HOUR

The ninth hour
is here

The ninth hour
makes no sense

The ninth hour
rises up wearily
in a freezing mist.

I have come to a river
of blood and vinegar

I have come to a river
where only pain
keeps its feet

I have come to a bridge
of dissolving bone

I have come to a place
of burning cold

I am trapped in a space
deformed
by my own
leprous fear

have I the strength
to pay suffering its due?

*   *   *

There is a calm
that is no cousin
to courage

There is a calm
that sits
like a quivering ape
under the python's
hypnotising eye.

Everything makes you
shiver

The hot wind. The rank river.
The poisonous euphoria.

But it's your shrivelling
flesh
that has the whip hand

Your flesh
has its own tumorous
will

You may think
you have been here
before

You may think
your quicksilver spirit
has your furtive flesh
licked

But darkness
is stronger
than light

The flesh knows best
who'll win line honours
in this fight

*　　*　　*

The ninth hour
is here

The ninth hour
makes no sense

Don't pray
for a flash flood
delivering miracle
or clarity

During the ninth hour
reason dies of thirst

Your blood stagnates
stale
as a base metal
in your mouth

You dangle
in a cacophony
of retching noise
with no grandiose riffs
of heroism

You will never forget
the foul sound
of the ninth hour.

*   *   *

I have come to a river
of blood and vinegar

I am here,
ninth hour,
I am here
stripped and shivering.

But listen, ninth hour,
listen
and pay heed
to a new sound
in me

I am not here
silent and alone

Do you hear
the fighting hiss
of this geyser
in me?

I stand my ground
in the undaunted spray
and company
of my own words.

NUMBERS

I get magic
    (sometimes I get more
        than I bargain for)

but I don't get
    numbers.

Numbers do worse
    than humiliate
        or elude me

they don't add up.

I am no algebra tart
    ravished
by the meretricious music
    of the spheres.

My eyes and nose
    never streamed
        with incontinent ecstasy
            through geometry classes
        as my disastrous triangles
            collapsed in a cacophony
                around me.

Perhaps it's a failing
        to grasp
            or even want
the utterly perfect number
        burning through my retina
like the utterly perfect morning.

Instead I peer
        with nauseating vertigo
into the deep dark pitch
        of numbers
like an exhausted mammoth
        dangerously tottering
            on the edge
                of a bottomless mystery.

THE HAMPSTEAD HEATH TOAD

For Roger Deakin

It was one of those
beautiful
English summer nights.

The lilac shimmer of silent
lakes.
The whisper of ghost fox
through your heartbeat.

But the toad in the hand
stank real.

Stank through his palpitating
skin.
Stank of fear.

Is the fabled hallucinogenic
touch of toads
just as Macbeth
witnessed
a hypnotising snare
of toxic apparition?

What thrilling doors of perception
open
to the musky ooze
of panting paralysed
terror?

Of course
intoxicated on moonshine
you wanted
and will always want
the toad
to calm down
smell sweet
and give up his phantasmagorical
secrets
generously.

But the toad in the hand
protected himself.

The toad in the hand
stank real.

CHARLES BAUDELAIRE'S GRAVE

How do you bury a poet?

Surely not
how they buried Baudelaire
thrown in with his parents
like an infant death.

It stretches
to a ghastly irony
Pasternak's remark
that poets should remain
children.

Do poets really want to trade
the lingering savour
of experience
for guileless eyes?

There's something
repulsive
about an empty fresh
adult face.

Such baby faces
can be seen in uniform
or with a foot
on a slaughtered tiger.

They can be capable
of anything
or a long lullaby
of nothing.

I want to exhume Baudelaire
and give him his own
magnificent mercurial vault.

From one angle
an arching ebony cat.
From another
sneering black marble
spleen.

No poet
dead or alive
should rot
with their parents.

EARLY MORNING AT THE MERCY

This six a.m. moment
in the cool-blue cool
of early morning
is not eternal.

It will pass
like the faint bat squeak
of an early bird call.

It is silent again
even as the dark
fades
and the white eyes of buildings
emerge
slowly gleaming
as they drop their grey veils.

But now the birds
are getting serious.
More and brassier
calls
as my first cup of tea
chills.

And I turn back
to Gwen's poetry
wondering
how on earth she could write
so eloquently in hospital.

Her spirit
must have been
as raucously persistent
as the dawn crowing chorus
of her vicious adored
golden roosters.

Or she was cheating –
and the *Bone Scan* poems
were written
when she was well
and safely remembering
her Plague Year
as she put on the kettle
and set out her shining
pens.

MULTIPLEX

Every night
  MULTIPLEX
shines through my hospital
  window

big blue neoned letters
    aimed vertically
at the thick dark sky
    like a rocket
      steadying its nerve
        on a launching pad.

Hiya, MULTIPLEX.
  Whoever you are
  you look like
    you're going places.
Take me with you.

ODE TO AGATHA CHRISTIE

Is this the crucial clue?
The bug-like trilobite
I bought from a slippery gypsy
in Prague,
still staring through its crystalline eyes
from the floor of an extinct sea.

I am spooked
by the abysmal depths
of my own life's mystery.
Like a belly-up Christie village
I'm nipped by the red herrings
of every pyrrhic victory.

Can I pocket and know this sunset
flaring over the rollers
of the cold Bass Sea?
No photograph, no poem
will make it anything
but a still-born cliché.

Is murdering time
the most true and convincing
perfect crime?

I tangle in the plot
chasing the hit-and-run driver
of my careless past tense.
Why does my childhood swimming pool
now stagnate darkly
behind a high wire fence?

I rub my clever egg head
and show off my waxed
moustache.
O Agatha, what fun playing
Poirot
to douse my fear in farce!

But how can I make
my solution ship arrive?
To what shimmering port
will it take me?
Or is it just an easy exile
from blind faith and wishful talk?

Death Comes as the End –
Agatha, you threw out cosy
when you served up dread.

As surely as my trilobite
with the right time, place
and gritty clout,
may I be preserved
as insoluble enigma
when a killer comet snuffs me out.

THE BEE HUT

For Robert Colvin

There is a dark place
on my friend Robert's farm
that thrums
with the nectar smell
of danger.

A swarm of bees
has taken over
a dozing old shed
and no one
has the means
or guts
to move them.

I think of slaughtered
Mycenean kings
entombed in their brick
hive
glittering as they lie
golder than honey
in the old blood
dark.

Entranced
my bare hand
wants to plunge
through a hole –
now a buzzing lethal
highway –
in the shed wall.

I love the bee hut
on my friend Robert's farm.

I love the invisible mystery
of its delicious industry.

But do I love the lesson
of my thralldom
to the sweet dark things
that can do me harm?

SMELLING TIGERS

THE SNOW LINE

I could smell
the snow line
but I just kept
talking

talking
and climbing
with this
glimmering
young man
who was talking to me
about death
how
a good dose of death
if you truly drink it
is a gift

a gift
a fresh cold
slap
a fresh dark
creek
you'll never sleep-walk
through your life
again

again
I wonder now
as I wondered then
in the seeping ambrosia
of pine trees
if I was climbing
effortlessly climbing
if I was talking
effortlessly talking
with a god

a god
who never touched me
or told me
his name
a god
of sweet chill
mountain air
sense
a comradely god
of wing-booted
presence.

SMELLING TIGERS

Waiting.
Starched hospital gown.
Frozen present tense.
Why am I smelling
tigers?

Muffled white noise.
Bleached magazines.
Why am I sniffing
the steaming black scat
of tigers?

When I get my life back
When I am clear of here
I will go
like a blind blessed arrow
where I can wallow
in the elixir
of tiger.

NOT THE SAME

When you climb
out a black well
you are not the same

you come to
in the blue air
with a long sore scar
circling your chest
like the shoreline
of a deep new sea

your hands are webbed
inviting you
to trust yourself
in water stranger
and wilder
than you've ever known

your heart has a kick
your eyes have
a different bite
you have emerged
from some dark wonder
you can't explain

you are not the same

THE SEA HARE

Don't bargain
    I tell myself
    as I scoop up the stranded sea hare
    gasping on the hot dry rock.

Can it hurt me?
    I know nothing about sea hares.
    Do they too make desperate deals
    with their deathless invertebrate gods?

Eerie to carry
    like an extraterrestrial
    yellow-green marooned jelly snail
    heavy in my towel.

Can it hurt me?
    Just bless and release it
    and fight the urge to count
    your sticky Karma beads.

Don't bargain.
    Just grab the swishing tail
    of your nerve's latest adventure
    and go with the inevitable tide.

You know nothing
    about sea hares
    but you know the prayer
    of your own shivering gut.

And it's bargaining   bargaining
    for the sea hare   for the sea hare
    and the future of both
    our unknowable lives.

ON NORFOLK ISLAND WITH BRUCE

This time last year I was on chemo
And bald in a week
Then another shock came out of the blue
To tell me you'd died in your sleep.

Too sick and groggy to go
Stunned to your funeral
Instead I raked the sky for your soul's bird
From the walls of my fumarole.

Now I'm here and healthy
Among the huge Norfolk pines
That wander like friendly free-range cattle
Through so many of your Manly lines.

I'm carrying your last book
Everywhere like a love affaire
A potent amulet against all my ghosts
That fret my gut with dead cold air.

Suddenly a local kingfisher flashes
Like a blue lightning crack
Through the salt-scoured stones of this cemetery –
I know it's you, Bruce, electrically back.

And I stand with my new hair
On unearthly fire
Under the tail of your azure comet
Watching you burnish this transient sky.

SPEARS

For F.H.P.

I know what I want
as I walk
through this valley
of Unknowing
I want my spears

my lost   my burnt
spears

these bright birds know
these strange trees
      must hear me
I want my spears

I cannot conquer
the past –
      the bonfire. the sealed shed.

Too late to strangle
      dead bigots.

But
never again
if my spears return
will a filthy fire touch them
never again
will their sanctuary
be ransacked.

Yes   I am a man
        without cover
but now ready
        with my old
        young man's
glory

I will have my life
        ceremonial
        sacred
I want my spears.

NIGHT RAIN

You have never slept
under night rain
spiritually tip-tapping
on a monastery roof.

Chinese Sung poets
wisely
would save
this kind of saturating
tranquillity
for withdrawn old age.

Night rain
for the unwithered
isn't always
a muffling lullaby.

Remember
that night the black sky
came roaring for you.
Ravaged awake
you lay quivering
under rain
like a bestial meteor shower
bloodying the roof.

It was astral
shock.
Your heart nearly
stopped.

Some night rain isn't meant
for enlightening
pensioners.

FOGGY WINDOWS

You can't preserve love
behind foggy windows

believe me
when your back is finally
turned
she steps out
shakes herself down
does her lipstick
and walks away
perhaps with an insouciant
swing to the hips
that would hurt
if you insisted
on looking back
if you regretted
not shackling her
in your car forever

but you don't want to spend
the rest of your life
blubbering in torn pieces
like Orpheus
or tasting a toxic dollop
of Lot's wife
on congealing cold eggs

so you don't fight it
you don't fight
love's right
to wind down
your precious
foggy windows.

RIMBAUD

For Michael Brennan

O saisons, o châteaux!
why did I stop
reading Rimbaud?

At twenty I was
convinced
I could read
to the rippling
roof
of seerdom
and jump.

There were so many things
I didn't yet know
about life, about Rimbaud.

I didn't know
you can grow
a grey immunity
to the most ardently
poisonous magic.

And that an older
even reliably dissolute
seducer
like Verlaine
so easily becomes
more foolish leech
than infernal lover.

Instead I ate caramel
ice cream
with those
as bullet-proofed
safe
as I was.

There are some things
reading poetry
can't deliver
or fix.

O saisons, o châteaux!
what illuminating
what absolutely necessary
Season in Hell
did I miss?

THE HORSEHEAD NEBULA

I was in Barcelona
late one Spring
when an insistent twilight
smoked me out
of my monastic hotel room
into the street.

I found myself
snared by the feral smell
of some amazing strange music
pulsing like a bull-ring
with singing and stamping.

My shy feet
were their usual lead
but I felt each rap
from the dancing crowd
reverberate in my breast
as if my own heart
were breaking into sparks
on a white-hot anvil.

There was only one dancer
who truly mesmerised me –
an aristocratically pale
young girl
caught in the rip of the music
as she dragged one foot behind her
in a misshapen boot.

I stayed
until dark
when the music stopped
and the dancers
slipped away.

I live my life
to live these moments
like living in waiting
for the smell
the uncanny smell
of the star-scorched flank
of the horsehead nebula
as she rises
in a stampede of hot music
from my boot-dragging dark.

WATERVIEW STREET

In the street
of my childhood
nothing is reliable.

My parents' friends are dead.
Their children gone.
Familiar houses
are dissolving.

I'd welcome the macabre
solid comfort
of cemeteries and weeds
but instead
there is a tropical
rotting splendour
that disturbs and distracts
like an invisible cockatoo
shrieking from a tree.

Time is melting
everything I remember
into a soft silt
shifting under the mud-mangrove
smell of the bay.

While I wait
for the eternally salty water
to unanchor all my memories
and sweep my old self away.

NEANDERTHALS

There's a deep warm cave
inside of us
where a last remnant
of Neanderthals
still lives

this is not an elegy
nor has deluded nostalgia
won another day

they were always repulsive
to us
and we were poison
to them

but we never wanted them
utterly gone
not before they told us
who they were
and why they knew
the dead must be blessed

we disturbed them
with their hands red
not from a bloody run-in
with a giant bear or each other

we disturbed them
with their hands ochre-red
preparing their dead

bigger and shiny-skinned
we yowled, threw smart stones
and gnawed their marrow-rich
inferior bones

we did dreadful things
we learnt nothing from them.

*　　*　　*

What was I trying to learn
whose bones was I gnawing
as I sat last week
on the bottom steps
of my old friend's
empty rotting mourning
house
crumbling down into the water
of my childhood's ancient mangroves?

I rocked on the salty tide
of the oyster-rimmed bay
alive and ageing and sad.

And I waited
for one of the Old Hairies
to brave the long hard climb
out
and teach me how
to rest my dead
and keep burning.

VAMPIRE

Each new ghost in my life
        living and dead
smells of mulch

a compost growing
        rich and strange
sometimes attracting
        a lyrebird
that rifles through it
        singing like a chainsaw
through its punctured neck

THE WATTLE BIRD

Until this morning
I've been woken up
by a red wattle bird
flinging himself
at the glass
of my half-open window
calling throatily
with raucous cheek
as he prances the wood
of my balcony rail

I'm old enough
to be flattered
and take no courting attention
for granted

this grey morning
I fumble awake
groggily trailing
cobwebs of a dream
about my long dead
still adored Siamese
clutching her to my frantic
dream self
as if she were, miracle,
still alive

this dry morning
of a slippery rainless winter
I sip my strong coffee
and listlessly watch
the window
longing for the joyous noise
of my new, if just
rattling through,
boyfriend.

EARLY MORNING BALLOONS OVER MELBOURNE

Unearthly in the chill blue
    they hang silent, coldly lovely
until there's that lurching
    belch of gas fire

and suddenly
    they're everything I'm afraid of –
heights, ice, other people in rocking space,
    my own helpless helpless
        fragility.

Why, when I dream of danger,
    can I never just reach out
        and grab
          the rising feet
            of a phoenix?

THE FOREIGN FOREST

You burn your bridges
going into a foreign forest
like a gleaming cruel
new school
where you don't know
the bluffing bullies
from the silent cougars.

You learn from experience
going into a foreign forest
where cold pine needles
have a smell
like a new lover's hair
in winter –
slippery ice spiced.

You can't name the flowers
going into a foreign forest
but the leaves blaze
against the early snow
like a moment-fire
blowing into your eyes
hot. too much. cold.

JERUSALEM

I. MY RIGHT HAND'S CUNNING

Sulfurous Psalm 137
yowling to the scarred harp
of exile
pledges my right hand's
cunning
if I forget Jerusalem

if I forget if I forget

but what does my right hand
know or remember
as my left hand gnaws
its bleeding friendless useless knuckles?

II. DAVID

When I think of David
I don't think of a skinny clapped-out
senile king
growling over the juicy young bones
of his latest concubine –

nor a hot-eyed paunchy poacher
of lesser men's wives,
the remote-control murderer
if the cuckolds are a bother –

nor a father sobbing
over his beloved hair-strangled enemy
and eldest son –

nor a shining darling
pledging himself to Jonathan
with the amulet of his breath –

nor Jerusalem's poet-in-waiting
lulling black-dogged Saul
with the narcotic of song.

When I think of David
I crave to be his favourite
and swing too
that psalm lasso
that caught and held forever
a remote hard god's pleasure.

III. MY YOUNG NOSE

Jerusalem has one delicious smell –

a fried chickpea
raucous savoury

cooked in tantalising mouthful balls
it sizzles aroma from grubby stalls

suffused with donkey and camel
my first taste of street falafel.

IV. HEROD

There's a touch of the Herod
in my half-breed face.

Like him I don't belong
in this priest-ridden place.

I hang fancy palaces from the cliffs
of my fortress lair.

Our enemies are fanatics.
They breed like rats.

Chancer mongrels both
we know how to behave
we burn, we slave.

V. TOPHET

At all the gates –
countless and terrifying –
the enemy gathers.

Moloch is sulking.
Is it wrong to ask our best
to bring their first born
to the Valley of Hinnom?

Moloch's burning-bronze gorge
our only deliverance.
And if overnight the enemy
did suppurate and die
in their plague-struck tents,
were we wrong to feed our god?

Remember us fairly
for Tophet, the place of fire.

Tophet, our purifying blood price
abyss.

How can you
who follow in peace
and wallow in righteousness
name our sacrifice
an abomination?

We didn't break our hearts
for God
we incinerated them.

Know this –
We too adore
our children.

VI. CRUSADERS

They don't like us.
They won't marry us.

We bury ourselves
catacomb deep
in high sterile castles.

Splinters of the True Cross
burrow like pious worms
under our nails
and fester.

At dawn we cough up gobs
of our own blood
not the pure Blood of the Lamb.

Allah's hostile breath smells
mint-tea fresh.

Our sodden homesick faith
makes us stink.

VII. GETHSEMANE

the bloody bastards
when your friends get pissed
and fail you
the bloody bastards

even God needs
short 'n' sweet ugly speech
when His friends fail Him

is it always worse at night
the long thorn hours
the hurt, the thirst?

the flowers may open
in their fragrant night sweat
the moon may glow full
on her Pesach bright trek

but Godhead is heartless
the Cup just can't be passed
to a single mortal one
of those bloody bastards.

VIII. CHURCH OF THE HOLY SEPULCHRE

When priests are pressed for space
when priests are greedy for grace
it's safest to stand clear.

When I was eighteen
I followed the incense
into a waxy-dark Coptic den
where a grimy cunning hand
blessed my breast
with a pinch of holy water.

Over the pernicious mourning stone
I was conned and robbed
of something precious of my own.

IX. THE STONING OF STEPHEN

One of the harshest judges unknowingly
grabbed a nob of meteorite
to hurl at Stephen.

A good shot,
it shattered the shining young man's
eye socket,
spraying through his skull
galaxies of heresies and alien bugs.

Was the new martyr's bloodied vision
impossible
or just extraterrestrial?

X. THE NIGHTINGALE IN MOLOCH

Is the secret frolic
in the heart of suffering
the nightingale in Moloch?

The bird looks like nothing.
The bird sounds like no one.

Moloch is a pine forest
on roaring resin fire.

Did some fierily distant Jewish clown
watch with a little long-view drollery
when witless Gentiles tore the Temple down?

XI. MOHAMMAD'S HORSE

The Anglican churches of my childhood
had an indelible smell –
varnished pew
blent with the Old Spice freshness
of my young father's half-Jewish
beautiful head
bent over a prayer book.

On its holiest of holy mountains
Jerusalem's gleaming Dome of the Rock
still holds the faintest faintest
fragrance –
amidst all the incessant sectarian human
squall –
of a horse, Mohammad's horse,
with a sweet horsey sweat on its impatient neck,
lifting off the Rock for Heaven.

One star-rushing night I leapt
from the cold silky stone floor
of the Sisters of Zion,
I left the ancient
Roman street
where the soldiers teased
mysterious Jesus,
I flew over my years to come
where I live and change
in bone and blood.

I flew in the smell
of Jerusalem,
I flew in unknowing flood.

AFRICA

SOME BIRDS OF AFRICA

Hornbills are dinosaurs gawking from thorn trees.
Flamingos are petals flocking around a crater lake.

The eye devours a lilac-breasted roller.
The heart is wooed for life when a fish eagle whistles.

The soul needs white-backed vultures.

WAITING FOR THE CROCODILES

At last
  I have the appetite
to make a meal
  of this stenching carcass.

I will glut
  dizzy with necessity
on its bloated guts
  then pick it sweet
and clean.

But its skin
  buffalo-tough
defeats me.

I need patience
  the patience of a vulture
waiting in the ruffling
  putrid breeze
for the kindly crocodiles
  to come and rip
this dead thing
  right open.

KUSINI CAMP

'A badger on my moment of life'—TED HUGHES

I too saw a badger
　on my moment of life
but not dead on an English road
　like Hughes' fly-blown beautiful animal
(why are Hughes' poem-creatures
　　always dead, dying or dazzling dangerous?)

My badger was African.
Nothing *Wind in the Willows*
　about him as he emerged
　　　suddenly
from an inhospitable termite mound –
　　as small mammals do
in the late afternoon
on the parched Serengeti.

Very much alive
　and on a wild animal's hungry mission
my badger lumbered
　　fluidly
through a shimmering dusk world
　　　of presences I could only glimpse
and now so hungrily
　　　remember.

THE FISH EAGLE

Even when David Livingstone
    was dying
he couldn't stop loving
    Africa

the Africa that made his name
    but killed his wife
      and broke his health
still sated him
      with rapture

rapture
    that had never left him
      after he was shaken
        like a mouse
          in the lion's mouth

the blessed mouth
    that mauled his arm
  and killed
    his fear of death

death in the heat
  death in the swamp
    death in his own inevitable
    weakness

in death's weakness
Livingstone wrote of the nearness
        of God
in the gleaming fecund world
        of dangerous wonder
burning him up
        in rapture

in dying rapture
    without a dreg of fear
he felt nothing but
        restless gratitude

gratitude in finding
    exactly the god-given word
to take with him forever
        the call of the fish eagle
            hanging high over the
            beautiful pestilent river
                        unearthly

WOLFGANG

In the Smithsonian
    specimen brains
        of inferior human species
            float in tanks
                like grainy fish.

The Wet Collection –
    a century old
        wrong turn
and fascinating
    embarrassment.

All the poems I've written
        after my trip to Africa
float in my own tank –
    Heart of Cuteness
where I hoard and ogle
        wondrous birds, magnificent
            mammals, sublime empty
            landscape and no
                Africans.

Why am I now conjuring
    Wolfgang?

The banal truth –
we were white tourists.
He was our shy driver-guide
with the charming colonial name.

But for me
   Wolfgang dominates the heart
   of one cold Serengeti
      dusk.

Wolfgang's soft tentative English
      blurs
         under the clapped-out
           safari jeep engine
as we bump bump bump
      along the rutted
         bone-littered savannah
           searching for cheetahs.

Wolfgang wheels us past
         bat-eared foxes and silver-backed jackals
          staring from termite-mound dens.

Wolfgang cranks
    our necks skywards
      to vultures clotting
      the branches
        of a lone umbrella tree.

We thrill
   to his sharp eyes
     and gifts of surprise …

Am I redeemed?

Or is Wolfgang's
   proud scalp
      now my tank's most authentic
       pickled star?

THE FREAK SONGS

*A song cycle written for performance
with the music of Jonathan Mills*

THE MALE SEAHORSE

Sung with passionate pride by a
conspicuously pregnant male seahorse

I brew
the impossible

I hold
the impossible

eggs! eggs!
that grow that grow
in my swelling male
belly

I hatch
the impossible

me
the pulsing star
exploding!

I float through
the impossible

the mess   the mess
the milky mess
of fathering

I am racked through
the impossible

my pain!   my pain!
squirts my brood
into the water

What does
the impossible
tell me
tell the world?

What sacred puzzle
have I unfurled?

What freak mystery
swells me
with wild wild joy?

THE WINGED HUMAN

Sung with bitter disillusion by a man
with uncontrollably flapping wings

Wings, you took advantage

Wings, you promised
the earth

Wings, you promised
the face of God

Wings, you said
I would feel his holy breath
through my hair

But like any seduction
you were just
a cloud castle

You promised me
ecstasy

You fluttered prettily
like swan's down

You told me nothing
but dangerous lies

Because now
I flap
in terror

Because now
my feet don't
know me

And can't fly
a straight line

Wings, turn me around

Wings, my freezing blood
is longing
to be earthbound

Wings, you took advantage

And now I fly
in fear and trembling

Wings, you promised
the face of God

And now
And now I fly
like a kicked sod

You promised
you promised
you promised
the earth

You promised
the face of God.

THE FRUITS OF ORIGINAL SIN

Sung with yearning by a suited man
with a dripping peach for a head

The fruits of Spring
are in the sinning

The smells of Spring
send my blood spinning

The tastes of Spring
make my juices roar.

Where will this
sweet rotten season
lead me?

Will a golden snake's kiss
enslave
or free me?

The fruits of Spring
are in the sinning

The smells of Spring
send my blood ringing

The tastes of Spring
make my juices
soar.

My heart
a spitting passion
fruit
I waft
in this luscious air

The bright red apple
hisses like a bright fire
and sings to me:

The fruits of Spring
are in the sinning

Where will the seeds
of my lush paradise
sprout?

The smells of Spring
send my blood spinning

To what peach poison
is my nose
stringing me?

The tastes of Spring
make my juices roar

I bite the apple
I lick the fire
I kiss the sweet sweet snake

I die by the sweet Spring's
sword.

CAT WOMAN

Song of seduction by a woman
dressed in a red latex cat-suit

Purr and claws
Purr and claws

Like a smoking ghost
I pass through walls

Purr and claws
Purr and claws

My nine lives
floating like gossamer
through the caressing air

Purr and claws
I always land
on your paws

I am your silky
black magic
I am your gentle teasing
death

let the witch
dribble my name
through her tortured
cries

let the witch
call for me
call for a gentle
teasing death
through the agonising
fire

Purr and claws
Purr and claws

I am your
silky black magic
I am your gentle
teasing death

you're lonely
without me
you long for my
wild soft breath

Purr and claws
Purr and claws

Be my willing slave
I'll be your burning
chore

I am your
silky black magic
I'm the gentle teasing
death
you want and adore.

THE VEILED LADY

A slow prayer sung by an enormously fat
woman with a bag over her head

Lord God
I am my most nakedly
yours

when you can't see my face.

Lord God

I am most open
to the slice
of your gaze

when you can't see
my face.

Lord God
Lord God

are you teaching me
a shame
that burns like grace?
when you can't see
when you can't see
my face.

Lord God
I live like a worm
in this dark.

Lord God
my foul and bloated
flesh
pleads for your sweet
surgery

are you teaching me
to love
a shame
that burns like grace?

when you can't see
when you can't see
my face.

IMAGINATION

Sung with hypnotising allure by a counter-tenor
dressed in very dirty black silk pyjamas

I'm your real world

I'm your bottomless pool
of sucking
black mud

trust me
trust me
I'm so soft and warm
and dirty

trust me
trust me
you can sink
so sweet and safely
right to the calling
and calling
bottomless
of me

I promise
I'll make the journey
worth your while

trust me
trust me
the dark and fabulous
things
you'll learn and know
from the dissolving roots
of your hair
to the soft slow burn
of your lost lost
toes

the dark and fabulous
things
I'll show
will never leave you
will never let
you go

I'm your real world
your bottomless pool
of black and sucking
mud

I'll seep right
through you
I'll change forever
your bones, soul
and blood

I'm your real world

trust me
trust me
I'm so soft and warm
and dirty

trust me
trust me
take my journey
take the plunge

you can sink
you can sink
so sweet and safely
right to the calling
and calling
bottomless
of me.

THE BLUEBIRD OF DEATH

A woman is dressed as a metallically glittering bluebird.
Her breasts end in sharp points, each breast like a
raptor's beak. She sings with a relaxed, deadly irony.

You live your life
as if you and I
share some sweet
understanding

You live your life
as if there's a secure cage
for my clipped wings
you're planning

You live your life
as if some gullible god
gave you the upper hand

You live your life
as if you can hold me down
and suck me bland.

(Threatening change of mood and tempo)

Don't fool yourself
my love
Don't kid yourself
my darling.

Sniff the air
Test the weather.

Smell the storm
of burning feathers.
Smell the storm
of our terrifying
flight together.

The day we go
you won't know

The place we go
you won't know

You'll learn, my love,
you'll learn, my sweet,
you'll learn
your bluebird
is not your lover
is not your mother

You live your life
as if you and I
share some sweet
understanding

You live your life
as if there's a secure cage
for my clipped wings
you're planning

Sniff the air.
Test the weather.

Smell the storm
of burning feathers
Smell the storm
of our last and final
flight together.

The day we go
The place we go

Only I will know
Only I will know.

LUCKY

TRAVEL

Waiting on a reeking strange
    railway station –
then the dead-quiet but crowded
    night ferry.

What country
    did I travel from
when I was born?

What alluring bait
    made me leave?

William Blake
    as he was dying
craned forward
    towards a country
he'd always wanted to see.

His rapturous curiosity
    always
        an unsettling inspiration.

The Venerable Bede
    embroidered his metaphor
        of the brevity of life
after watching
    a sparrow fly
        from one darkness to another
        a living flash
through a torch-bright hall.

What lives
    keep leaping
      to and fro
those pregnant black tunnels
      of being?

On a bold day
    my own footloose
      soul
can smell a good
      sailing wind –
the dare
      in Blake's shimmying-up-the-mast
last breath –
and then crawl
  snug and wide-eyed
    into the downy
    undercarriage
of Bede's plucky
    traveller bird.

SISTER-IN-LAW

For Jenny

Until I met you
I always believed
I lived in an outlaw's space
where family remote or close
could only be
blood or ghetto

and any gay,
determined to make
their own way,
will tell you straight –
blood is no reliable
home
nor fix
against intolerance.

Until I met you
I was content
to keep my Melbourne family
simple.

my lover. my cat.
my books.

Jenny, believe me
my cosy grumpy cocoon
had not planned
for a sister-in-law
as sweet, as insistently
inclusive as you,
to release me from my own
lonely prejudice too.

LUCKY

For Andy

There's a damp melancholy
in T'ang poetry
that smudges
the lovely jade
precision.

I love Walt Whitman's
spunky company
but under his bardic
whistling
I can hear his lonely heart
howling
at the turned back
of some deaf rough trade.

So many poets
starve
in the cold faery spaces
between their frost-bitten ears.

How lucky I am
to hear you, darling,
coming up the stairs
to smell the coffee
floating ahead of you
like my favourite incense.

FOSSIL FERNS

For Rachel and Sam on their wedding day

When the shy garden
    of fossil ferns
indelibly inked
    in my sandstone path
was frond-green
    and under dinosaur foot
it was a hotter different world.

Things change –
    but some beautiful things
    even in their changing
    wondrously remain.

Like the magical space
    that love creates
where strange
    even fabulous
    plants can grow –
not to mention
    a thundering hungry reptile
    or two.

I won't say
         best of all
         the humble fern –
I like a pterodactyl
         in the hand
         as much as any girl –
but how lovely
         to watch over a lifetime
         these exquisite fern amulets
             unfurl.

LAST ARIA FROM *THE ETERNITY MAN*

From a chamber opera composed by Jonathan Mills

I always knew
Eternity would smell
Like a cold salt wind

I always knew
Eternity would be
A wild   a wild
sea

A wild sea
That will climb
The highest cliff

A wild sea
That will growl
Through the rocks

A wild sea
That will hiss
From the deep

A wild sea
That will come
When I call

A wild sea
I will hear
And smell
Like a lover finally
Climbing
In the window
I would never open

A wild sea
Coming wave after
Blue-black wave
For me.

Oh my valley of briny vision
Take me
In your salty arms!

Let my own soul's tide
Rise and Flood
And rejoice.

*　　*　　*

How can I write
On water?

Do the fish
Do the giant squid
Read?

How can I write
On water?

There is only
One mortal place
Left

No angel is ever
Unadorned
To go before
His maker.

VIEW FROM 417

The sky – twilight sky –
is a wisping blue
friendly and unearthly

I'm not sure where I am

The buildings my window
lets in
have an art deco look
of white flat squares
with art deco design
flourishes
exorbitantly flamboyant
for a hospital room
landscape

Something in me
despite everything
can't believe my luck

26 November 2008,
Mercy Private Hospital, Melbourne, Room 417

Index of First Lines

Index of Titles